CERTAIN
PEACE
IN UNCERTAIN TIMES

Shirley Dobson

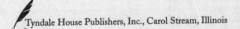

Tyndale House Publishers, Inc., Carol Stream, Illinois

Visit Tyndale's exciting Web site at www.tyndale.com

TYNDALE and Tyndale's quill logo are registered trademarks of Tyndale House Publishers, Inc.

Certain Peace in Uncertain Times

Previously published in 2002 by Multnomah Publishers, Inc., under ISBN 1-57673-937-6.

First printing by Tyndale House Publishers, Inc., in 2008.

Designed by Jessie McGrath

The Library of Congress has cataloged the original edition as follows:

Library of Congress Cataloging-in-Publication Data

Dobson, Shirley, 1973–
    Certain peace in uncertain times / by Shirley Dobson.
        p. cm.
    ISBN 1-57673-937-6
    1. Prayer—Christianity. I. Title.
        BV215.D63 2002
        248.3′2—dc21

ISBN-13: 978-1-4143-2150-9
ISBN-10: 1-4143-2150-3

Printed in the United States of America

14   13   12   11   10   09   08
 7   6   5   4   3   2   1

Dedication

I lovingly dedicate this book to my family. First, to my precious mother, who brought peace and love into our home during troubled times and whose prayers have sustained me all these years. Also, to my stepdad, Joe, who with his contagious smile brought laughter, fun, and stability to my life when I needed it most. He is a treasure. And to my only brother, John, who has been my lifelong friend.

To my wonderful husband, Jim, who continues to be God's greatest love gift to me and who has brought happiness, adventure, and excitement to my life. After forty-seven years of marriage, I think it's going to work!

Last, to my two children, Danae and Ryan, whom I deeply love and count it a privilege to pray for daily. May they run with perseverance the race that is set before them, looking to Jesus, the pioneer and perfecter of their faith (Hebrews 12:1–2).

Thank you all for the many ways you have blessed my life.

Acknowledgments

I want to express my appreciation to Bill Muir, who created the acrostic P.R.A.Y. that provided the foundation for this book.

To the members of my incredible National Day of Prayer Task Force, who relentlessly urged me to write a book on prayer for the encouragement of those who desire a richer and deeper prayer life.

To my husband, Jim, who despite his busy schedule squeezed in time he didn't have to offer his suggestions and counsel.

To Don Morgan, who sharpened and polished the manuscript and made it more readable.

To Donna Greene, my personal assistant, who handled with patience and grace the many details related to this project.

To Bill Berger, who served as a liaison between my publisher and me and made many other valuable contributions.

And to Don Jacobson and all my friends at Multnomah, and Jim Lund in particular, for his talent and expertise in the careful and final editing process.

Finally, to the Lord Jesus Christ for His daily strength, guidance, and steadfast love.

Table of Contents

Foreword

Dear Reader,

This little book, *Certain Peace in Uncertain Times*, will help you discover a life-changing gift. It's one God wants especially to give His people in times of uncertainty and suffering. Although it comes wrapped in anxiety, the gift itself—a breakthrough in your prayer life—is a treasure.

I hope you read every page of Shirley Dobson's book with great anticipation. You'll find tremendous insights from a woman who has made prayer a lifelong passion, and who has become an inspiring prayer mentor to thousands.

You should know that you are part of a tremendous nationwide movement toward prayer. Perhaps this renewed interest arises from the unusual challenges we face. When the horrors of September 11 unfolded, people gathered by the thousands. To do what? To pray. Longtime ministry friends in Washington, D.C., tell me they have never seen more leaders on Capitol Hill meeting simply to pray. The president himself recently said that the remark he hears most often as he travels the country is "Mr. President, I want you to know I'm praying for you."

The very fact that you're reading this now means, I believe, that God is at work in new ways in your life.

You should expect and prepare for significant personal change. In fact, if you're like many who read my book *The Prayer of Jabez*, you're about to make a shocking discovery—that God delights to answer a specific prayer in a specific way for you. Of course, most Christians believe in prayer in a general sort of way. But you're about to find out from personal experience that God wants to hear from *you*—your praises, your confessions, your innermost thoughts, your urgent requests. He is waiting for you to open your heart to His love and leading—and He's poised to answer your prayers in ways you've never before imagined (Ephesians 3:20).

Keep reading, and keep praying. Your life will never be the same. And neither will your world.

God bless you on your journey!

BRUCE WILKINSON
WALK THRU THE BIBLE MINISTRIES
ATLANTA

Preface

Are you afraid? Do you often worry? Are you sometimes so anxious that you don't even want to get out of bed in the morning?

In today's tumultuous times, we all have moments like these—myself included. But there is an antidote for this anxious age. It connects us to the greatest source of peace, hope, and security that we could ever imagine. The cure is a remarkable gift from our loving and merciful God. It's called *prayer*.

I'd like to share with you how prayer works, and how important it is to God. In this little book you will discover a four-step approach to prayer known as "P.R.A.Y." You'll also find a thirty-one-day devotional filled with wonderful examples of how to apply the P.R.A.Y. method. But most of all, you will see how talking to God has changed my life—and how it can change yours.

Won't you join me?

Chapter 1

Searching for Peace in an Anxious World

The phone was ringing. I tried to blink sleep out of my eyes and focus on the clock next to my bed: *midnight.* I picked up the receiver.

The woman on the other end of the line was hysterical. Through tears, she told me that she was a single mother living in California with her three young children. She was having a panic attack. Over and over she told me, "I can't cope—I can't deal with all this!"

This young mom is not alone.

Most of us are struggling to cope with "all this." We are members of an increasingly stressed-out society. According to one researcher, one-third of the U.S. population experienced a panic attack in the last year.

More than 19 million Americans suffer from debilitating anxiety disorders. *Harvard Business Review* has reported that stress-related symptoms account for 60 to 90 percent of medical office visits. Our pharmacies can barely keep Maalox and Prozac in stock.

What is happening? Why do so many of us live in a continual state of fear and anxiety?

We each have our own set of reasons: Health problems. Marital difficulties. Parenting battles. Financial struggles. An amoral culture. Technological advances that accelerate the pace of life into a dizzying spin. Violence on our roads and in our schools. And most recently, threats of terrorist attacks in a variety of forms. Today, even the formerly mundane task of opening a letter can be a life-threatening event! I know of at least one mother who wouldn't let her daughter open Christmas cards for fear of anthrax exposure.

At the same time, some of us are contending with fears that stem from our past. I still remember the pain and anxiety I endured as a little girl, watching helplessly as my father's addiction to alcohol grew steadily worse. I didn't understand his erratic and sometimes volatile behavior, and I became ashamed of him and of our run-down home. There was not a single blade of grass in our front or backyard. Paint was peeling off the outside of the house and some of the rooms inside. I was too embarrassed to invite a friend over to spend the night. Millions of other children have experienced these same distressing circumstances.

Studies reveal that one-fourth of children in the world today live in an unstable or dangerous environment. When a boy or girl grows up in a home characterized by violence, physical abuse, sexual abuse, neglect, or any unhealthy behavior or attitude, he or she typically feels ashamed, humiliated, and insecure. I know firsthand that these feelings are not easily erased in adulthood.

Not everyone, of course, is struggling with troubles past and present. Yet even those who are "coping" often find it hard to relax today. After all, a crisis could be right around the corner. It seems to be one of the rules of living—just when we think we have our little world buttoned down, we encounter what a friend of mine calls a "suddenly."

A FRIGHTENING NIGHT

My husband, Dr. James Dobson, and I experienced a shocking "suddenly" on June 16, 1998. We had put in a twelve-hour day at Focus on the Family and the National Day of Prayer. I was too exhausted to cook, so Jim offered to fix me a hamburger.

We were in the kitchen. Jim was assembling the

burger and I was going through the day's mail. Suddenly I heard the burger hit the floor. I glanced up and saw Jim slowly trying to locate the meat with his foot. I said, "Jim, what are you doing?" He didn't answer. I repeated the question, and again he didn't answer.

I looked into Jim's unfocused eyes and realized that he was unable to speak. Then he reached out, put his arms around me, and held me tight.

Panic-stricken, I ran to the phone and dialed 911. Within minutes the paramedics were rushing Jim to the hospital. He had experienced a major stroke. That began the most frightening night of my life, as he underwent two CAT scans and other diagnostic tests. The neurologist then told me about a recently developed medication called tPA that could be very helpful. The downside was that death occurs in about 6 percent of patients who receive it. I had to make the decision whether or not to administer the drug. What a terrifying moment that was!

That began the
most frightening
night of my life.

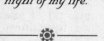

Knowing that Jim would rather take the chance on wholeness, I decided to authorize the medication. Six other people had to sign the release, which absolved the neurologist and the hospital of liability. The tPA was administered just forty minutes before the end of the three-hour period beyond which it becomes ineffective. Still, Jim couldn't speak, and his right side was partially paralyzed.

I faced the prospect of losing my beloved husband of nearly four decades, or, if he survived, of helping Jim through years of speech therapy, physical rehabilitation, and medical care. As I drove home from the hospital at 5 A.M., I began praying. I was experiencing one of the greatest challenges to my faith in my entire life. I wondered why the Lord would take away the abilities to write, speak, and create from this gifted man who ministered every day to millions around the world. As Jim had written in one of his books a few years earlier, there are times in our lives when God doesn't appear to make sense. This was certainly one of them for me.

Little did I know that He was about to perform a wonderful miracle for Jim. When the news of Jim's stroke was announced on Focus on the Family's radio program and millions of people around the world began to pray for him, God clearly heard and answered their (and our) petitions. Later that morning, Jim began to say a few words, and by 4 P.M. that day he was essentially over the stroke. He talked in sentences and his strength returned. He suffered no disability, and today, four years later, he is more creative and effective than ever.

Tragedy does not always end this miraculously, even for those who have served the Lord faithfully for many years. God is sovereign, and He does what is best in His eyes. Yet even when the worst occurs from a human perspective, "God works for the good of those who love him" (Romans 8:28). Prayer is never unanswered. Sometimes the response is *yes*, sometimes it is *no*, and sometimes it is *wait*. But our heavenly Father is there even in the most troubling of circumstances.

You may have encountered a crisis of your own recently; you may even be in the midst of one right now. When these "suddenlys" strike, they are unnerving reminders of the fragility of our existence.

We all want peaceful lives and contented hearts. Yet with threats to our tranquility growing at a seemingly exponential rate, is it any wonder that many of us succumb to worry and fear? More important, is there a solution? *Can* we know certain peace in these uncertain times?

The answer, of course, is *yes*.

OUR REFUGE AND STRENGTH

Though some might christen the twenty-first century the Age of Anxiety, our current troubles are not new. Mankind's future has always been uncertain. Since the days of Noah and his family, Moses and the nation of

Israel, the persecuted early church, the Pilgrims, and America's founding fathers, the answer for people facing adversity has always been the same: Almighty God.

Simply put, there is no security apart from Him. When problems threaten to engulf us, we must do what believers have always done—turn to the Lord for encouragement and solace. As Psalm 46:1 states, "God is our refuge and strength, an ever-present help in trouble."

Because of our pride, or affluence, or independence, or a thousand other reasons, many of us act as if we can get along just fine without the Lord. For years we've put up a sign that says to God, "KEEP OUT! Keep out of our government. Keep out of our communities, businesses, and entertainment. Keep out of our schools. Keep out of our families. Keep out of our lives!"

And God is gracious. He doesn't force His way into places where we have not invited Him. He politely leaves us alone, taking His shield of protection and peace with Him. The psalmist informs us that "the shields of the earth belong to God" (Psalm 47:9, NKJV). When those shields are removed, we face the fury of life's storms on our own.

Yet God does not abandon us. He keeps His promise: "Never will I leave you; never will I forsake you" (Hebrews 13:5). Even during the storms, He stands just to the side, ever watchful, waiting to embrace us the moment we again seek His presence. His words to Jeremiah apply to us all: "Call to me and I will answer you" (Jeremiah 33:3).

Even better, our Father reveals *how* we are to call upon Him. We can speak directly to heaven through a remarkable gift called prayer.

THE LIFELINE OF PRAYER

I learned to depend on the Lord early in my childhood. During those turbulent years, my mother held our little family together. Though she wasn't a Christian at the time, she knew that she needed all the help she could get as she raised her children. So she sent my brother and me to church every Sunday, and it was there that I was introduced to Jesus Christ and invited Him into my heart.

As I learned how to pray and began speaking to the Lord, I sensed His love and care for me. Amid the chaos of our disintegrating family, this little girl found hope and comfort in Jesus. I've been praying and relying on Him ever since.

The many answers to prayer in my life have reinforced my belief in its power and importance. Prayer is our pathway not only to divine protection, but also to a personal, intimate relationship with God. That's why I am so honored to be in my eleventh year as chairman of the National Day of Prayer Task Force. I count it a privilege to play a small part in calling people of faith to their knees.

Jesus demonstrated the significance of this intimacy with God to His disciples. He "often withdrew to lonely places and prayed" (Luke 5:16). He "went out to a mountainside to pray, and spent the night praying to God" (Luke 6:12). He even told the disciples the parable about justice for the persistent widow "to show them that they should always pray and not give up" (Luke 18:1).

I have often wondered why the Bible places such a heavy emphasis on prayer, especially since Jesus reminded us during the Sermon on the Mount that "your Father knows what you need before you ask him" (Matthew 6:8). When I mentioned this to my husband, his response was both simple and profound: "Well, God desires a *relationship* with each one of us, and there is no relationship in eavesdropping!"

"There is no relationship in eavesdropping!"

Indeed, the Lord desires a personal, two-way conversation with me—and with you. You are His child. He wants you to seek Him, to love Him, and to spend time daily with Him. When you do, He hears and responds. Jesus said: "When you pray, go into your room, close the door and pray to your Father, who is unseen. Then your Father, who sees what is done in secret, will reward you" (Matthew 6:6).

If Christians would follow through on this truth, we would change our lives and the course of history. After all, just as prayer is important for us as individuals, it is also important to entire nations. One of my favorite Scripture verses is 2 Chronicles 7:14: "If my people, who are called by my name, will humble themselves and pray and seek my face and turn from their wicked ways, then will I hear from heaven and will forgive their sin and will heal their land."

As I reflect on this verse, I am encouraged. Prayer groups are springing up throughout America. Our nation's leaders are openly asking for prayerful support from the public. As a matter of fact, for the first time in more than a century, members of both houses of Congress met recently in the Rotunda of the U.S. Capitol for a time of prayer and reconciliation. In the midst of our tumultuous times, God may be preparing hearts for a new openness to seeking Him through the lifeline of prayer.

How about you? Are you ready to renew or increase your own commitment to prayer? Do you want contentment in your heart and peace in your world? If your answer is *yes*—or even *maybe*—I encourage you to keep reading. I will introduce you to the National Day of

Prayer's four-step approach to effective communication with God. It's simple, practical, and biblical. We call it P.R.A.Y.—Praise, Repent, Ask, and Yield.

The apostle Paul urged that "requests, prayers, intercession and thanksgiving be made for everyone . . . that we may live peaceful and quiet lives in all godliness and holiness. This is good, and pleases God our Savior" (1 Timothy 2:1–3). Let's please God by actively seeking, through prayer, "peaceful and quiet lives"—for ourselves, our spouses, our children and grandchildren, our friends, and our nation.

Are you ready to know certain peace in uncertain times? Good. It's time to P.R.A.Y.

Chapter 2

P ~ Praise

Giving Glory to God

A few years ago, Jim and I attended a University of Southern California football game. On a beautiful Saturday afternoon we entered venerable Los Angeles Memorial Coliseum and settled into our seats, enjoying the anticipation of a festive afternoon. Thousands of fans joined us, many displaying the latest in USC apparel. The marching band performed several popular tunes. Then a regal Trojan warrior appeared astride a white horse. The warrior thrust his sword skyward; together, man and horse charged across the field to the roar of the crowd.

The stage was set. At one end of the field, a huge mass of players in cardinal and gold uniforms and helmets huddled together. The crowed buzzed expectantly. Suddenly, the players raced en masse toward the center of the field as the band burst into the USC fight song. The crowd (two Dobsons included) rose as one and delivered a thunderous ovation for the young heroes. Fans clapped, raised their arms, and voiced their admiration at the top of their lungs. The power and enthusiasm of that greeting must have been heard for miles!

I don't remember many details about the game itself. But I do recall the conversation that Jim and I had afterward about our collective display of adoration. For thousands of us, the exhilaration we felt when the USC team ran onto the field was total and genuine. But a question nagged at me: If we can respond like this to a group of college student-athletes, how much more awe and enthusiasm should we be willing to show to our heavenly Father?

In any discussion of this nature, it's important to remember that God is not our "genie in a bottle"—He is not simply waiting in heaven to receive our laundry list of self-centered requests. On the contrary, God is worthy of our praise and is pleased when we come before Him with thanksgiving. He wants to be appreciated, just as we do.

Praise and adoration are not merely "appetizers" in the lives of believers—they are part of the main course. David, who gave us so many wonderful words of praise in the Psalms, put it this way: "Ascribe to the LORD the glory due his name.... Worship the LORD in the splendor of his holiness" (1 Chronicles 16:29).

In the same way, praise and worship are essential to an effective and satisfying life of prayer. When Jesus taught His disciples how they should pray, He *began* with praise: "Our Father in heaven, *hallowed be your name*" (Matthew 6:9).

We would be wise to keep this in mind when we pray. After all, our God is the sovereign Creator of the universe! He loves us as His own children and has provided every good thing we have; He is worthy of our praise every moment. Yet I know that many of you are facing frustrations and trials and sorrows that threaten to overwhelm you. Your hope and faith are still in the Lord, but right now you just don't *feel* very worshipful. You may be thinking: *Shouldn't I wait until the feeling returns to offer Him my praise? Isn't that more genuine?*

God is worthy of our praise every moment.

Here is my suggestion: Instead of waiting for the feeling, wait upon God. You can do this by growing still and quiet, then expressing in prayer what your mind knows is true about Him, even if your heart doesn't feel it at this moment. Be honest. Tell the Lord how much you need His presence in your cold, empty heart to rekindle and ignite your praise for Him. In faith, invite the Lord to fill your heart—then wait until He does.

When we make this sincere effort to give our hearts

and minds to God, we draw near to Him—and He draws near to us, just as He promised (see Hebrews 10:22–23). We begin to taste His refreshing water that soothes our inner thirst. We start to see how perfectly capable He is of handling our cares and concerns, which suddenly seem much smaller. We finally relax and focus fully on praising and trusting Him.

INSPIRATION FOR ADORATION

There are other ways to rediscover adoration for the Lord. The most obvious source is the pages of Scripture. The Psalms, especially, are filled with marvelous descriptions and examples of praise to our heavenly Father. Psalm 89 begins, "I will sing of the LORD's great love forever; with my mouth I will make your faithfulness known through all generations."

We can also turn to songs of praise in a hymnbook, as well as to many excellent books that explore God's character and attributes. Of course, worshiping with fellow believers at church can be a tremendous source of inspiration. Setting aside regular family times for praise and worship may also bring out heartfelt moments of heavenly acclamation.

In the Dobson household, one of our favorite traditions at both Thanksgiving and Christmas has been for family members to share at least one blessing from the past year for which they are especially thankful. It is a time for appreciating each other and God; typically, many of us are in tears before we're done! These moments always remind us just how much God has given us all.

Author Ruth Myers writes, "I find that my worship is richer when I offer the Lord praise and thanks for three things: *who He is, what He does,* and *what He gives.*"

At this very moment, what can you say about each of these? I urge you to review often the questions of who God is, what He does, and what He gives. I pray that your answers every day will be a little richer, a little stronger, and a little more powerful in the grip they hold on your heart's affections.

THE PLEASURE IS HIS

God is most worthy of our praise—yet we have another reason to worship Him. He invites us into conversation with Him because it brings Him *pleasure.*

> *God actually delights in and pursues our worship.*

That's sometimes a little hard to believe, isn't it? The holy and perfect and all-powerful ruler of the universe *enjoys* our prayers of praise? But the proof is in Scripture: "The prayer of the upright is His delight" (Proverbs 15:8, NKJV). God actually delights in and pursues our worship. As Jesus said, "A time is coming and has now come when the true worshipers will worship the Father in spirit and truth, for they are *the kind of worshipers the Father seeks*" (John 4:23).

It always thrills my heart to read those verses! It is overwhelming to think that when I worship Him in spirit and truth, God is actively seeking *me*. That brings an excitement to my worship, whether in church or in private prayer.

When you build on the enthusiasm that grows from this kind of worship, your entire life can become a song of praise to God. In His perfect plan, your existence in this life, and for all eternity, will bring Him glory just as He promised. You can even say, as David did, "I will praise you, O Lord my God, with all my heart; I will glorify your name forever" (Psalm 86:12).

Scripture promises that the whole of creation will be filled with His glory. In this very moment, today, your praise to Him can be part of that glory. By speaking to Him, by singing, even by worshiping Him in adoring silence, you and I can offer our very own praise to Almighty God. What an honor and privilege!

THE PLEASURE IS ALSO OURS

The pleasure of our praise and prayers will always be God's—but there is indescribable pleasure in these acts for us as well. Our worship is more than a duty. It's a deed that generates a deeply satisfying joy.

It's actually quite striking to see how closely joy is linked with prayer in New Testament teaching:

> Be *joyful* in hope, patient in affliction, faithful in prayer. (Romans 12:12)

> Be *joyful* always; *pray* continually; give thanks in all circumstances, for this is God's will for you in Christ Jesus. (1 Thessalonians 5:16–18)

> *Rejoice* in the Lord always. I will say it again: *Rejoice!* Let your gentleness be evident to all. The Lord is near. Do not be anxious about anything, but in everything, by *prayer* and petition, with thanksgiving, present your requests to God. And the peace of God, which transcends all understanding, will guard your hearts and your minds in Christ Jesus. (Philippians 4:4–7)

> In all my prayers for all of you, I always *pray* with *joy*. (Philippians 1:4)

No part of our prayers creates a greater feeling of joy than when we praise God for who He is. He is our Master Creator, our Father, our source of all love. Every breath we take is a gift from His hand. When we focus on Him, we move from being self-centered, with worry and distress, to being God-centered, with joy and peace in our hearts.

When you pray, praise our God of blessings with all your heart! But don't end your prayer there—it's only the beginning.

Chapter 3

R ~ Repent

Seeking His Forgiveness

I never fully comprehended the significance of lying when I was growing up. I knew that being untruthful was wrong, but I never came to terms with the moral implications.

I can recall many instances when boys asked for dates and I lied to them because I didn't want to go. It was better than rejecting them, I reasoned. I often lied to my mother when I was about to be caught or punished for something I had done. The implications of this sin did not come home to me until several years after I was married. It was a relatively minor offense that brought it to a head.

I went into the kitchen one day to fix Jim a tuna sandwich. He had hated mayonnaise with a passion ever since eating one mouthful too many as a four-year-old. I knew that but decided to sneak a small amount into the tuna in order to hold it together. I figured there was too little for him to taste, and I saw no harm in making the sandwich (from my perspective!) better.

When I served the plate to Jim, his first question was, "Did you put mayonnaise in the tuna?" Caught red-handed, I lied. I said, "I know you don't like mayonnaise. Of course I didn't put it in your sandwich." Jim ate his lunch without noticing a thing, but the incident bothered my conscience for days. Finally, I couldn't stand it anymore. I confessed.

To understand Jim's reaction, you have to know that lying had been a cardinal sin for him since he was a small child. A strong sense of right and wrong has been a hallmark of his character throughout his life. Jim knows that untruthfulness is an offense specifically condemned in Scripture (see Revelation 21:8 and Proverbs 6:17). He takes these verses literally and tries his best to live by them, even in regard to relatively insignificant matters.

Finally, I couldn't stand it anymore. I confessed.

Not surprisingly, Jim was very disappointed when I told him what I had done. Not only had I added the hated mayonnaise, I had lied to him point-blank. He told me, "A marriage must be built on mutual trust and truthfulness between a husband and a wife. If they are honest with each other about the little things, they will not deceive each other about the big things." At the time I thought Jim had overreacted, but now I see that he was attempting to establish a very important principle in our marriage. We had a long talk about our relationship and committed to each other that lying would not be part of it.

What came after the "mayonnaise incident" was not only an improvement in our relationship, but also a greater understanding of honesty and what God expects of us. I asked God to forgive me for lying to Jim, and for my tendency as a youth to distort the truth. I have attempted to live by a higher standard from that time.

Repentance is the aspect of prayer that believers seem to shy away from most often. But look at its value! Our relationship with the Lord, and our continuing communication with Him, is dramatically improved by this act of cleansing. The same truth applies to every other relationship in our lives.

When we repent, we obey Scripture's command and open the way to experience the exciting promise that accompanies it: "Humble yourselves before the Lord, and he will lift you up" (James 4:10).

Often, repentance means confessing our failure to live as God wants us to. These failures may take the form of outward acts and words, but an unholy attitude requires repentance just as much. "Man looks at the outward appearance, but the Lord looks at the heart" (1 Samuel 16:7).

STEPS OF REPENTANCE

I believe that repentance has three components.

First, we must recognize what we've done wrong and why it's wrong. The classic example of this occurred when Nathan the prophet confronted David about his adultery with Bathsheba and his murder of her husband, Uriah. When Nathan was finished, David immediately admitted his sin without any excuses. The first time I read this passage in 2 Samuel 12, I felt that David must have fallen on his knees before the echo from Nathan's words even died away.

Second, in repentance we must be truly sorry for our sin, and we must express our intent to turn away from it. "Godly sorrow brings repentance" (2 Corinthians 7:10). In David's repentance prayer in Psalm 51, he wrote, "The sacrifices of God are a broken spirit; a broken and contrite heart, O God, you will not despise" (v. 17). For the apostle Peter, after he had denied Christ three times, repentance meant that he went off by himself and wept bitterly (Matthew 26:75). Yet from this low point Peter went on to an incredible ministry as a witness for the Lord.

Third, we must show willingness to make amends,

plus willingness to do whatever we must to avoid repeating the sin. The example of Zacchaeus, the tax collector whose house Jesus visited, reminds us that when righting our wrongs is possible, the Lord expects us to do so. Zacchaeus proved how sorry he was by volunteering to return four times as much money as he'd taken from anyone he had cheated.

Full and true repentance is literally an about-face. It means turning completely around, *away from* sin, and turning *toward* God.

EFFECTS OF REPENTANCE

I believe that the faithful practice of repentance has at least three important results.

First, it allows us to remain in the fellowship of God's presence. "If we confess our sins, he is faithful and just and will forgive us our sins and purify us from all unrighteousness" (1 John 1:9).

Second, repentance encourages our honesty before God. In David's prayer in Psalm 51, he tells God, "Surely you desire truth in the inner parts; you teach me wisdom in the inmost place" (v. 6). Even while he was coming out of his sin and accepting God's cleansing, David recognized the standard of integrity God holds us to.

Third, repentance allows healing in our souls. When

our body has an open wound, we first clean it to prevent infection and promote healing. Repentance removes old sins and wrong attitudes and opens the way for the Holy Spirit to restore our spiritual health.

Repentance opens the way for the Holy Spirit to restore our spiritual health.

I have experienced this restoration and healing many times in my life, but one of the most deeply felt was a day many years ago that our family now calls "Black Sunday."

As is true for many families with young children, the Sunday morning "get 'em ready for church" routine was often chaotic in the Dobson household. But this Sunday was uniquely so. Jim and I got up late, which meant that all of us had to rush to prepare for church. Spilled milk at breakfast and black shoe polish on the carpet added to the tension. Finally, Ryan, who was dressed first, managed to slip out the back door and get dirty from head to toe. At least one spanking was delivered that morning, and another three or four were threatened.

That evening Jim and I called the family together. We described the day we'd had and asked each person to forgive the others for their part in it. We also gave each family member a chance to express his or her feelings.

Finally, we prayed as a family, asking God to forgive us and to help us live and work together in love and harmony. It was an invaluable time of communication and honesty that drew us even closer than before.

REPENT EVERY DAY?

Theologians have differing perspectives on the definition of *sin* and on whether or not true believers need to ask for reconciliation and forgiveness continually. Some contend that we sin every day in word, thought, and deed; whereas others suggest that sin is a deliberate transgression of a known law of God and that human failures and faults do not require the same contrition as do acts of flagrant rebellion.

Whatever your understanding might be, it is clear that we should always maintain an attitude of submission to the will of God as we interpret it in our lives, confessing our sin whenever the Holy Spirit leads us to do so.

Here's what Elisabeth Elliot had to say about this issue:

> Sometimes it happens that I can think of nothing that needs confessing. This is usually a sign that I'm not paying attention. I need to read the Bible. If I read it with prayer that the Holy

Spirit will open my eyes to this need, I soon remember things done that ought not to have been done and things undone that ought to have been done.

Speaking personally, I attempt daily, and even hourly, to maintain very short accounts with the Lord. My ultimate purpose in living is to hear these words when I stand before Him in the life to come: "Well done, good and faithful servant!" (Matthew 25:23).

FORGIVENESS

In the model prayer Jesus gave us, He taught us to say to God, "Forgive us our debts, as we also have forgiven our debtors" (Matthew 6:12).

So often for us, repentance will mean *forgiving*. God commands us not to retaliate for personal grievances, not to hold grudges, not to be resentful or bitter. But it happens so easily! I believe that forgiveness can become a continuing cycle—because God forgives us, we're to forgive others; because we forgive others, God forgives us. Scripture presents both parts of the circle.

For example, Jesus tells the story of the unmerciful servant whose master turns him over to be tortured. Then Jesus adds a warning: "This is how my heavenly

Father will treat each of you unless you forgive your brother from your heart" (Matthew 18:35).

Paul touches the other side of the circle when he writes, "Bear with each other and forgive whatever grievances you may have against one another. Forgive *as the Lord forgave you*" (Colossians 3:13).

Because we repent, we're forgiven. Because we're forgiven, we're to forgive. And because we forgive, we're given the grace to recognize that it's already time to repent again!

Chapter 4

A ~ ASK

Expressing Your Needs to Him

Of all the aspects of prayer, "ask" is probably the one with which we can most easily identify. Who hasn't asked for something from our heavenly Father?

The truth is, we are remiss if we *don't* take our requests to the Lord. Jesus Himself taught us to pray, "Give us today our daily bread." But our Father encourages us to seek more than care of our physical needs. He wants to hear and meet our requests for spiritual and emotional fulfillment, too.

I remember a night when the Lord answered one of my urgent requests in a most tangible way. The kids, then quite young, and I were alone in our home; Jim was traveling. I was sleeping peacefully until suddenly, about 2 A.M., I awoke with a start. I didn't know why, but I was filled with fear!

I lay in bed for several minutes (it seemed like hours) and worried. Finally, I forced myself out of bed and sank to my knees.

"Oh, Lord," I prayed, "I don't know why I'm so frightened. I ask You to watch over our home and protect our family. Send Your guardian angel to be with us." I climbed back into bed. The fear had subsided somewhat, and a half hour later I was asleep. But in the morning a neighbor came over and said that a thief had broken into our next-door neighbor's home. The police had determined that the burglary occurred at 2 A.M.—the same time I had awakened in fear!

The Lord protected us that night through my anxious prayer.

"If a burglar wanted to break into *our* house," I said, "he'd probably try to get in through the bathroom window near our children's bedrooms. Let's go look."

We checked that side of the house and saw that the window screen was bent and the windowsill splintered. Someone had indeed started to break in. But what had stopped him?

I'm convinced that the Lord protected us that night through my anxious prayer. God not only answered my plea in a literal sense by stopping evil at the gate, but He also gave me the peace I needed to go back to sleep and leave matters entirely in His hands.

Peter says, "Cast all your anxiety on him because he cares for you" (1 Peter 5:7). Our heavenly Father does care for us and desires to meet our needs. But for our own good—for the development of our active, healthy dependence on Him—He invites us to *ask* Him for these needs to be met. According to James, "You do not have, because you do not ask God" (James 4:2).

God makes prayer as easy as possible for us. He's completely approachable and available, and He'll never mock or upbraid us for bringing our needs before Him.

All He asks is that we make our requests known to Him.

GUIDELINES FOR ASKING

God tells us a great deal in Scripture about how to bring our requests before Him. This is obviously something He wants us to do often, for His own pleasure as well as for our well-being.

- *Ask in Jesus' name.* Jesus told His disciples, "Until now you have not asked for anything in my name. Ask and you will receive, and your joy will be complete" (John 16:24).

  Asking in the name of another means that someone else has granted you the authority to submit a request in his name. More specifically, this person wants you to make a petition on his behalf. So, by asking in Jesus' name, we're making a request not only in His authority, but also for *His* interests and *His* benefit. Understanding this should revolutionize our commitment to prayer!

Praying in the name of Jesus also means coming to God on the merits of Christ rather than on our own qualifications. We're not worthy of even a moment of the Lord's time or attention, but Christ has infinite worth in His Father's eyes. Opening a prayer in Jesus' name is like visiting a powerful king and presenting a letter of introduction from an especially important nobleman; this letter allows you an unlimited claim to the king's attention and unrestricted access to his kingdom.

- *Ask while abiding in Jesus.* Jesus gave His disciples the image of a vine and its branches as a picture of His relationship to them (see John 15:1–6). He then said, "If you abide in Me, and My words abide in you, you will *ask what you desire,* and it shall be done for you" (v. 7, NKJV).

As a child, I was introduced to Jesus by Mrs. Baldwin, the Sunday school teacher in my little neighborhood church. She described Him as my special friend, and thereafter I sought a closer relationship with Him. I began praying about the struggles inherent to living with an alcoholic father. I asked for a change in my father—and if he wouldn't change, I prayed that God would protect our family and give us a father who would love and take care of us.

The Lord had not forgotten the prayer of a hopeful little girl.

My family disintegrated when I was in the sixth grade. My parents divorced, and my mother, brother, and I moved to a tiny "shoebox" of a house. But the Lord had not forgotten the prayer of a hopeful little girl. My mother soon met and married a wonderful man who became a devoted father, faithful husband, and good provider. They are now in their nineties and have lived together harmoniously for more than fifty years. This was the first of countless prayers that the Lord has answered decisively on my behalf.

From my first introduction to Jesus as a little girl, my relationship with Him grew steadily—as did my commitment to prayer. I believe that a fruitful prayer life begins with a total abiding in Christ, an alive and flourishing union with Him.

- *Ask according to God's will.* Jesus teaches this emphasis in His model prayer from Matthew 6:10: "Your will be done on earth as it is in heaven." The apostle Paul tells us that the will of God is "good, pleasing and perfect" (Romans 12:2). We must keep God's perfect will in focus as we make our requests.

  Following this guideline doesn't restrict our asking; instead, it builds our confidence in prayer. "This is the confidence we have in approaching God," the apostle John writes, "that if we ask anything according to his will, he hears us. And if we know that he hears us—whatever we ask—we know that we have what we asked of him" (1 John 5:14–15).

  We approach God, we ask within His will, and we *know* that He hears. This is our wondrous privilege as God's children!

- *Ask in faith.* We can clearly see the requirement to have *faith* in the instruction James gives us for requesting wisdom:

  > If any of you lacks wisdom, he should ask God, who gives generously to all without finding fault, and it will be given to him. But *when he asks, he must believe and not doubt,* because he who doubts is like a wave of the sea, blown and tossed by the wind.

That man should not think he will receive anything from the Lord. (James 1:5–7)

The certainty of answered prayer comes through even more strongly in the words of Jesus. "Ask and it will be given to you; seek and you will find; knock and the door will be opened to you. For everyone who asks receives; he who seeks finds; and to him who knocks, the door will be opened" (Matthew 7:7–8).

When my children were young, I began praying and fasting for them on a weekly basis, a practice I continue to this day. I believe that over the years these prayers have protected them from many dangers, particularly during a six-month period when we almost lost one or the other on four separate occasions. There is *power* in faithful prayer. I would never have been able to keep up my commitment to pray and fast for my children if I didn't believe wholeheartedly in their effectiveness—and in the awesome authority of Almighty God.

There is power in faithful prayer.

* * *

- *Ask with thanksgiving.* "Do not be anxious about anything," Paul tells us, "but in everything, by prayer and petition, *with thanksgiving,* present your requests to God" (Philippians 4:6). This "thanksgiving" is the inevitable—and sometimes overwhelming—result of our faith in God's answers to our prayers, and our faith in God's loving control over every aspect of our lives.

- *Ask with right motives.* "When you ask," James tells us, "you do not receive, because you ask with wrong motives, that you may spend what you get on your pleasures" (James 4:3). If our prayers aren't answered the way we want, it doesn't necessarily mean that our motives are wrong—but we can be sure that asking God to stretch, bend, or manipulate His laws to fit our selfish desires or circumstances will lead to an unfavorable response.

THE SCOPE OF OUR REQUESTS

When the Holy Spirit comes to dwell within us, I believe we gain a built-in inclination to take our concerns and needs to the Lord in prayer. Read again Paul's words from Philippians 4:6: "Do not be anxious about anything, but in *everything*…present your requests to God." *Nothing* qualifies for worry; *everything* qualifies for prayer.

By the same work of the Spirit within us, I believe we can learn to look beyond our personal situation to those around us—our families, our communities, our nation, and our world. God will instill His concern for others within our hearts so that we start to care for them as He does. Our prayers for them begin to flow more readily. We yearn for others to receive their salvation from His hand, to know His tender care as their Father and Friend.

This is one of the reasons for my involvement with the National Day of Prayer. I believe that this annual call to prayer is just one example of a way to extend our care and concern for all of God's children. As we open our hearts and prayers to God's leading, we join in His work around the world. This is what we were born for—or rather, *re*born for!

> *As we open our hearts to God's leading, we join in His work around the world.*

When we come before the Lord with praise, humbly repent of our transgressions, and in obedience present our petitions to God according to the guidelines set out for us in Scripture, He *will* answer. Our final task, then, is to yield to His perfect will.

Chapter 5

Y ~ Yield

Submitting to God's Will

Because of my own unsettled upbringing, roots are very important to me. As a young wife, I visualized always living in the same house in which I raised my children, growing old while watching my grandchildren play in the same tree house and sandbox our two kids had enjoyed.

But after nineteen years in the Arcadia, California, home that held so many warm and loving memories, my dream began to unravel. Our ministry, Focus on the Family, had outgrown its facilities, and the high cost of local property prohibited us from building a new campus in the area. Following much searching and prayer, the Focus board of directors selected Colorado Springs as our new home.

Though I knew this was a positive change for the ministry, I did not welcome it with enthusiasm. I found myself asking, *Why, Lord?* I felt I needed the support system we had developed in California. Our friends there saw Jim and me not as ministry leaders, but as "Jim and Shirley." We'd been in one another's weddings and had babies together. For years we'd had them over to celebrate the Fourth of July in our backyard.

I grieved to leave this safe and loving circle of friends and to say good-bye to my parents and both of our children. Jim said that when we moved I left skid marks all across the Rocky Mountains!

In Colorado, I continued to wrestle with feeling sorry for myself and missing home, family, and friends. Yet I still sought the Lord's direction. One day I was standing in the bathroom preparing for work when I felt His presence. "Shirley," He seemed to say, "I'm not concerned about your happiness; I'm concerned that you are in My will, and My will is that you be in Colorado."

From that point on a new peace filled my heart. The lingering feelings of discontent left me. Though I still miss my roots and friends, after ten years in Colorado

A new peace filled my heart.

———— ✺ ————

Springs, I can see God's hand in it all. I have stretched and grown in ways I couldn't have imagined. Over the years, my old friends have moved, too. Only a few of those couples still live in the same area of California, and we see our family almost as often now as before.

No matter how fervent our desires and requests, the Lord does not always respond the way we would choose. Sometimes His answers to our petitions are the very opposite of what we've sought—yet He always has our best interests in mind.

When Jesus said, "Come to me, all you who are weary and burdened, and I will give you rest," he added, "Take my yoke upon you and learn from me" (Matthew 11:28–29).

Coming to our Lord in acceptance and prayer requires us to also yield to His yoke. We must submit to where He leads and what He commands, even if He sends us in a direction we don't want to go.

It's a bit like river rafting with an experienced guide. You may begin to panic when the guide steers you straight into a steep waterfall, especially if another course appears much safer. Yet after you've emerged from the swirling depths and wiped the spray from your eyes, you see that just beyond the seemingly "safe" route was a series of jagged rocks. Your guide knew what he was doing after all.

When we yield to the Lord's leading, we discover the additional truth that followed Jesus' statements above: "I am gentle and humble in heart, and you will find rest for your souls. For my yoke is easy and my burden is light" (vv. 29–30).

What Christ offers is indeed a yoke, and we must indeed yield—yet when we do we are amazed at the lightness of the load, and at the inner peace we feel.

STRAIGHT PATHS

In submitting to the Lord's leading, we obey Scripture's command: "Trust in the LORD with all your heart and lean not on your own understanding; in all your ways acknowledge him" (Proverbs 3:5–6). At the same time, we open our lives to the promise that accompanies the command: "…and he will make your paths straight" (v. 6).

The path that Jim and I have taken over the course of our marriage is not one I'd planned on. I thought that I would be a teacher, Jim would establish a full-time Christian psychology practice, and later we would spend our lives in medical research. I am a private person who would have preferred a life outside the limelight, surrounded by family and friends.

I would have preferred a life outside the limelight. But God had something else in mind!

But God had something else in mind! Through Jim's books and speaking engagements, as well as many other unexpected developments, the Lord specifically called us to the highly visible world of Focus on the Family. Later, He showed me how I could serve Him through a role with the National Day of Prayer Task Force.

Even though we did not seek this life, we have always tried to discern and yield to His will. Jim and I believe that we are on the "straight path" that He wants us to travel, and we welcome it wholeheartedly. Our prayer now is to finish the race *strong*.

Yielding to the will of God is simply letting His Holy Spirit have His way in our lives. Continual prayer allows us to be "filled with the Spirit," as God commands us. Scripture declares that God's will for us is to "Be joyful always; pray continually; give thanks in all circumstances" (1 Thessalonians 5:16–18). If we yield, we will continually be filled with joy and thanksgiving in the Spirit.

REVERENT SUBMISSION

In yielding to God through our prayers—as in nearly every other aspect of the Christian life—Jesus is our example. Just before the Crucifixion, in Gethsemane, He offered the same prayer three times: "My Father, if it is possible, may this cup be taken from me. Yet not as I will, but as you will" (Matthew 26:39).

You and I may never understand what those moments meant for Jesus. However, a short passage in the book of Hebrews seems to refer to His time in Gethsemane:

> During the days of Jesus' life on earth, he offered up prayers and petitions with loud cries and tears to the one who could save him from death, and he was heard because of his reverent submission. Although he was a son, he learned obedience from what he suffered. (Hebrews 5:7–8)

One thing is clear: Jesus yielded Himself to the Father's will. He was a model of "reverent submission." Jesus lived a life of prayer, faith, and obedience.

INTENSELY PERSONAL

When we fully yield to the Lord, I believe that our prayer relationship with Him becomes intensely personal. At different times in my life, I have felt His hand guide me to choose wisely in the midst of uncertainty, to feel contented after a difficult experience, to gently probe further when discussing a problem with a friend, or to simply fall on my knees and pray. Those moments have come only when I have been consistent in making time for prayer and consciously seeking His direction for me.

The specifics of this personal communication vary for each of us, but the principles apply to us all:

- *Yielding means continuing to grow,* especially in understanding what the Scriptures say about every aspect of our lives. To achieve steady growth, we must read and obey the Word regularly.
- *Yielding means doing everything in Jesus' name.* In Colossians 3:17, Paul said, "And whatever you do, whether in word or deed, *do it all in the name of the Lord Jesus,* giving thanks to God the Father through him."
- *Yielding means growing in our ability to listen,* through the Holy Spirit, to the voice of our Lord as He guides us through our lives. Jesus said, "My sheep listen to my voice; I know them, and they follow me" (John 10:27). We listen, and we follow.
- *Yielding means undergoing a refinement process.* The refining of precious metals requires intense heat. Gold, for example, doesn't melt until it reaches a temperature of 1,945 degrees Fahrenheit (that's hot!). As the gold liquefies in a smelting furnace, unwanted properties called slag rise to the surface.

After cooling, the slag is chiseled away until only the purified metal remains.

Similarly, when we yield to God, the Master Refiner strips away the flaws and distractions that hinder intimacy so that we can unreservedly surrender our hearts to Him.

• *Yielding means abandoning ourselves to God in contented trust.* As Oswald Chambers said in *My Utmost for His Highest:*

Let actual circumstances be what they may, keep recognizing Jesus, maintain complete reliance on Him.... Be reckless immediately, fling it all out on Him. You do not know when His voice will come, but whenever the realization of God comes in the faintest way imaginable, recklessly abandon. It is only by abandon that you recognize Him.

As we discover new and deeper ways to yield, we develop a personal relationship with the Lord that transcends all other relationships. We begin to sense the love, power, and peace that only He can provide.

SPIRITUAL BATTLE

Several years ago, Jim served on the U.S. Attorney General's Commission on Pornography. More than ever before, Jim was fighting a tremendously profitable industry in a highly visible way, and the pornography kingpins were not happy. Our family began to face unusual "attacks," and I had a strong sense that we were in a spiritual battle against the forces of Satan. To counteract that, I bathed Jim and our children in prayer.

I suddenly had a strong urge to pray for Danae.

One rainy night, I was alone and working in the kitchen. I suddenly had a strong urge to pray for Danae, who was out with a friend. At first I ignored the impression, but it was so strong that I put down what I was doing and prayed right then for Danae's safety, calling for a legion of angels to protect her.

A while later, a policeman came to our home and told me that Danae and her friend had been in an accident on a mountain road. The car she was driving had hit a slick mixture of oil and gravel and flipped over, sliding on its top within a few feet of a five-hundred-foot precipice—a sheer drop-off with no guardrail. Both Danae and her friend suffered minor injuries, but neither was seriously hurt.

I can only conclude that the prompting I felt to pray was a "call to battle" from the Lord—and that when I yielded to this call with my petition to heaven, He allowed me the victory I sought. I can still picture those angels, standing wingtip to wingtip, providing a safe guardrail.

We are in a continual battle with the spiritual forces of evil—but we will triumph when we yield to God's leading and call on His powerful presence in prayer.

THE PEACE OF GOD

It may sound like a paradox, but even as we listen for God's call to combat evil, so we must also seek the heartfelt peace that comes from heaven. This means experiencing "the peace of God, which transcends all understanding," the peace that "will guard your hearts and your minds in Christ Jesus" (Philippians 4:7).

Lisa Beamer knows this peace. Her husband, Todd, was a passenger on one of the airplanes that were hijacked on September 11, 2001. When they learned that the plane was headed on a suicide mission for the nation's capitol, Todd and several of his fellow passengers made a valiant effort to take control of the craft. The plane went down in a Pennsylvania field—killing everyone on board, but sparing the lives of countless others in Washington, D.C.

Recently, Lisa expressed her thoughts on losing her husband in such a tragic way: "The choice for me is to either look at all the things I have lost or the things I have. To live in fear or to live in hope.... Hope comes from knowing I have a sovereign, loving God who is in every event in my life."

Three centuries ago in northern France, a theologian named Francois Fenelon, who won fame as a great "director of souls," taught about the importance of carrying prayer into daily action by constantly seeking and surrendering to this holy peace.

> Lay aside this ardor of mind which exhausts your body and leads you to commit errors . . . . Speak, move, act in peace, as if you were in prayer. In truth, this is prayer.

"Peace I leave with you," Jesus promised; "my peace I give you.... Do not let your hearts be troubled and do not be afraid" (John 14:27). The experience of this peace is something we can lay hold of in prayer and continue in by yielding to His power. It comes only through the super-natural working of the Holy Spirit.

COME FORTH AS GOLD

The rewards of yielding to God's will are many, but they are often hidden. Our prayers sometimes seem not answered at all. At one point in his life, Job's world seemed to be falling apart. He felt utterly separated from the Lord. Yet even in his misery, he still had the faith to say, "But he knows the way that I take; when he has tested me, I will come forth as gold" (Job 23:10).

We will all "come forth as gold" if we understand that God is sovereign and knows what is best, even when we cannot understand what is happening at the time. He asks us to trust Him and to know that He cares for us even when we can't track Him.

That assurance can be hard to accept, especially at times like the day we packed up all our belongings for the long trip to a new home in Colorado Springs. I felt then that I was abandoning everything I held dear. Yet even during those difficult moments, I was preparing myself to accept the perfect will of my Lord. I was comforted by the truth I had learned so many years before: God hears every one of our prayers, and He answers them in His time, according to His sovereign will.

If we humbly come before God with our petitions, He *will* show us what it means to have certain peace in uncertain times.

31 days to
P.R.A.Y.

Praise. Repent. Ask. Yield. These four simple steps can take our prayers beyond empty words of recitation to the kind of intimate, personal communication that our Lord so desires to have with His children. He is the Master Creator, our Father, the source of all love—and He wants a relationship with us. As we establish a deeper link with God in prayer, we will find the worries and fears of today slipping away. They will be replaced by the love and contentment that is only possible through Him.

I hope that the previous chapters have given you a sense of the joy, hope, and peace that are available to you through prayer. To help you make this approach a habit, I urge you to try the following 31 Days to P.R.A.Y. devotional over the next month. I believe it will enrich your prayer life and bring you closer to the Lord than you ever thought possible.

All God's blessings to you and your family!

Prayerfully yours,

PERSEVERE IN PRAYER

Jesus once told a story about a widow who repeatedly asked a judge for justice against an adversary:

> "For some time [the judge] refused. But finally he said to himself, 'Even though I don't fear God or care about men, yet because this widow keeps bothering me, I will see that she gets justice, so that she won't eventually wear me out with her coming!'" And the Lord [Jesus] said, "Listen to what the unjust judge says. And will not God bring about justice for his chosen ones, who cry out to him day and night?" (Luke 18:4–7)

Scripture says that Jesus told the disciples this parable to show "that men ought always to pray, and not to faint" (Luke 18:1, KJV). Let us never faint from the privilege of bowing before God in prayer!

P.R.A.Y. FOR TODAY
Praise God for His patient teaching on prayer;
repent of any "fainting" you've done when you've
failed to persevere; ask for His help to be faithful
in prayer in the midst of life's stresses;
yield to Him by joyfully persevering
even when you're tempted to give up.

Day Two

GOD'S WILL FOR YOU

Do you realize that you already know God's will for you today? Here it is: "Be joyful always; pray continually; give thanks in all circumstances, for *this is God's will for you* in Christ Jesus" (1 Thessalonians 5:16–18).

Prayer is our privilege of constant, unbroken communication with God. We can consistently talk with Him about everything. As Robert L. Thomas says, this continual prayer commanded in the Bible "implies constantly recurring prayer, growing out of a settled attitude of dependence on God. Whether words are uttered or not, lifting the heart to God while one is occupied with miscellaneous duties is the vital thing."

Incessant prayer, says Thomas, is "the only way to cultivate a joyful attitude in times of trial." It's also the best way to stay in tune with the perfect will of God.

P . R . A . Y . FOR TODAY
Praise God for His making His will so clear;
repent of any failure to be joyful, prayerful,
or thankful; ask for His help in being more
prayer-minded hour by hour;
yield to Him by letting go of any sulking
resistance to joy or thankfulness.

Day Three

OUR PRAYER EXAMPLE

In *The Master Plan of Evangelism,* Robert E. Coleman explains how Jesus showed through His prayer life how His disciples should live:

> Surely it was no accident that Jesus often let His disciples see Him conversing with the Father. They could see the strength which it gave to His life, and though they could not understand fully what it was all about, they must have realized that this was part of His secret of life. Note that Jesus did not force the lesson upon them, but rather He just kept praying until at last the disciples got so hungry that they asked Him to teach them... (Luke 11:1).

Don't you long for that hunger yourself? As you study the life of Christ, try to experience Him as the disciples did, and then let His example lead you to a life of holiness and strength.

P.R.A.Y. FOR TODAY

Praise God for Jesus' example of prayer;
repent of any dullness in learning from Jesus;
ask Him to continue teaching you; yield to Him today
by praying through His model prayer (Luke 11:2–4),
expanding each part with your own words.

FELLOWSHIP WITH GOD

In *Fellowship*, his devotional study of John's epistles, John G. Mitchell examines the fellowship with God that is ours through Jesus:

> The great yearning of the heart of God is that we should have fellowship with Him. The purpose of redemption is not just to free us from sin nor simply to get us to heaven, but rather to fit us for eternal, unbroken, wonderful, personal, intimate fellowship with the living God Himself.... Some people are waiting for fellowship, with its joy and peace, until they get to heaven. My friend, God wants us to have it now.... It is not that we are waiting to have fellowship with God, but God is waiting for us to have fellowship with Him!

You can have that kind of incredible, intimate fellowship with God right now by falling to your knees in prayer.

P.R.A.Y. FOR TODAY

*Praise God for the warmth of His fellowship;
repent of any ways in which you've turned your back
on Him; ask that others will experience His fellowship
today; yield to Him by talking to others about the value
of fellowship with God.*

THE CHRISTIAN'S LIFELINE

At one point in his ministry, Jim Cymbala, author of *Fresh Wind, Fresh Fire,* sensed that God had a message for him:

> If you and your wife will lead my people to pray and call upon my name, you will never lack for something fresh to preach. I will supply all…that's needed, both for the church and for your family, and you will never have a building large enough to contain the crowds I will send in response.

As the people's prayers were answered, the Cymbalas saw a wider application to the truths they were learning:

> Prayer is the source of the Christian life, a Christian's lifeline. . . . Pastors and churches have to get uncomfortable enough to say, "We are not New Testament Christians if we don't have a prayer life."

If you make that kind of commitment to prayer this very day, you too can connect to the source of Christian life and watch God supply all that's needed for you and your family.

P.R.A.Y. FOR TODAY
Praise God for being the Shepherd of your church;
repent of any failure to seek His power;
ask God for a breakthrough in your church's ministry;
yield by praying for this with others.

Day Six

EXPERIENCING GOD

In *Experiencing God,* Henry T. Blackaby and Claude V. King write:

> Your personal prayer life may primarily be one-way communication—you talking to God. Prayer is more than that. Prayer includes listening as well. In fact, what God says in prayer is far more important than what you say....
>
> Prayer is a relationship, not just a religious activity. Prayer is designed more to adjust you to God than to adjust God to you. God doesn't need your prayers, but He wants you to pray. You need to pray because of what God wants to do in and through your life during your praying. God speaks to His people by the Holy Spirit through prayer.... Genuine prayer does not lead to an encounter with God. It *is* an encounter with God.

Through prayer, God quickens *our* spirits by the power of His Holy Spirit. That's an experience we don't want to miss!

P . R . A . Y . for Today

Praise God for His eternal perfection;
repent of any attempts to adjust God to yourself;
ask Him to adjust you to Him; yield to Him by making
whatever changes are necessary.

PRAYER IN TIMES OF TROUBLE

We sometimes feel a bit ashamed to find that most of our prayers occur during severe hardships. Yet Martin Luther seemed to view the situation differently:

> Except under troubles, trials, and vexations, prayer cannot rightly be made. God says: "Call on me in the time of trouble"; without trouble it is only a bald prattling, and not from the heart; it is a common saying: "Need teaches to pray."

That's a strong statement! God certainly wants us to pray at *all* times, not just in moments of crisis (1 Thessalonians 5:17). But Luther makes his point—when times are good, our natural tendency is to drift away from God. Likewise, trials seem to bring out our most fervent prayers. Let's thank God for allowing troubles that drive us closer to Him.

P.R.A.Y. for Today

Praise and thank God for the burdens in your life;
repent of any failure to be grateful for them;
ask for His help in the specific difficulties you currently
face; yield to Him by not complaining.

PRAYER VERSUS SLEEP

In Gethsemane, Jesus "returned to his disciples and found them sleeping. 'Could you men not keep watch with me for one hour?' he asked Peter. 'Watch and pray so that you will not fall into temptation. The spirit is willing, but the body is weak'" (Matthew 26:40–41).

In *A Serious Call to a Devout and Holy Life,* William Law says:

> Prayer is the nearest approach to God, and the highest enjoyment of Him, that we are capable of in this life.… On the other hand, sleep is the poorest, dullest refreshment of the body…so far from being intended as an enjoyment, that we are forced to receive it either in a state of insensibility, or in the folly of dreams.

Sleep is essential, but prayer is even more important. Ask God to help you find the right balance in your life.

P. R. A. Y. FOR TODAY
Praise God for His grace in allowing you to talk with Him; repent of any drowsiness or dullness you've had in prayer times; ask for more of His spiritual energy; yield to Him by changing your prayer routine to help you stay alert.

PRIORITY OF PRAYER

In *Power through Prayer,* E. M. Bounds argues persuasively for making prayer a priority in our busy schedules:

> To pray is the greatest thing we can do: and to do it well there must be calmness, time, and deliberation; otherwise it is degraded into the littlest and meanest of things…. There is nothing which it takes more time to learn. And if we would learn the wondrous art, we must not give a fragment here and there—"A little talk with Jesus" as the tiny saintlets sing—but we must demand and hold with iron grasp the best hours of the day for God and prayer.

The manifold rewards of a serious, consistent prayer life demonstrate clearly that time with our Lord should be our first priority.

P.R.A.Y. for Today

Praise God for being above and beyond time;
repent of any failure to give enough time to prayer,
and for being too hurried in the time you did give;
ask for His help in being more efficient and effective in
your use of time; yield to Him by giving Him
the best hours of your day in prayer.

RED HOT PRAYER

Charles Spurgeon wrote this commentary on the apostle Jude's phrase, "pray in the Holy Spirit," from Jude 1:20:

> Praying in the Holy Ghost is praying in fervency. Cold prayers ask the Lord not to hear them. Those who do not plead with fervency, plead not at all. As well speak of lukewarm fire as of lukewarm prayer—it is essential that it be red hot.
>
> It is praying perseveringly. The true suppliant gathers force as he proceeds, and grows more fervent when God delays to answer.... Beautiful in God's sight is tearful, agonizing, unconquerable importunity.... We shall never sing *Gloria in excelsis* except we pray to God *De profundis:* out of the depths must we cry, or we shall never behold glory in the highest.

May your prayers be just as heartfelt—and as "red hot."

P.R.A.Y. for Today

Praise God for being a "consuming fire," as Scripture says; repent of being lukewarm in prayer; ask Him to make you powerful in prayer for the rest of your life; yield to Him by tossing aside your spiritual dullness and blazing forward in boldness and fervor.

PRAYING IN THE SPIRIT

Listen to Oswald Chambers on what it means to pray in the Spirit:

> The whole meaning of prayer is that we may know God. The "asking and receiving" prayer is elementary; it is the part of prayer we can understand. But it is not necessarily praying in the Holy Spirit.... Our minds must be saturated by the revelation of prayer until we learn in every detail to pray in the Holy Spirit. Prayer is not an exercise, it is life....
>
> The sign that the Holy Spirit is in us is that we realize that we are empty, not that we are full. We have a sense of absolute need...[which] is one of the greatest benedictions because it keeps our life rightly related to Jesus Christ.

Part of this "absolute need" is the joy of having the Holy Spirit residing within us. Once we have experienced His presence, we must have Him always.

P.R.A.Y. FOR TODAY
Praise God for being the source of all life;
repent of ever feeling falsely satisfied;
ask for a true awareness of your emptiness;
yield to Him in emptying yourself of any
pride or self-sufficiency.

Day Twelve

THE WELLSPRING OF LIFE

"Above all else, guard your heart, for it is the wellspring of life" (Proverbs 4:23).

Jesus expanded our understanding of this "wellspring" in the heart. "Whoever believes in me, as the Scripture has said, streams of living water will flow from within him" (John 7:38). Consider John Calvin's commentary on this passage:

> There can be no doubt…that they who believe shall suffer no want of spiritual blessings. He calls it living water, the fountain of which never grows dry. . . . Still he does not say that, on the first day, believers are so fully satisfied with Christ, that ever afterwards they neither hunger nor thirst; but, on the contrary, the enjoyment of Christ kindles a new desire of him. . . . The Holy Spirit is like a living and continually flowing fountain in believers.

We have the boundless privilege of tapping into that fountain every time we pray.

P . R . A . Y . FOR TODAY
Praise God for the flow of His Spirit in your life;
repent of any pollution; ask for His Spirit to cleanse
your heart; yield to Him by hungering and thirsting
for more of His presence and power.

SPIRITUAL ARMOR, SPIRITUAL PRAYER, SPIRITUAL BATTLE

After telling us about our need for spiritual armor in facing our enemy, Paul adds: "And pray in the Spirit on all occasions with all kinds of prayers and requests. With this in mind, be alert and always keep on praying for all the saints" (Ephesians 6:18).

Commenting on this verse in *How to Pray,* R. A. Torrey writes:

> Paul realized the natural slothfulness of man, and especially his natural slothfulness in prayer. How seldom we pray things through!… I wish the whole verse might burn into our hearts. But why is this constant, persistent, sleepless, overcoming prayer so needful? First of all, because there is a devil…and if the child of God relaxes in prayer, the devil will succeed in ensnaring him.

If an empty mind is the devil's playground, what better way to fill ours than with prayer?

P.R.A.Y. for Today

Praise God for providing you with spiritual armor through prayer; repent of any failure to take up this armor; ask Him to burn into your heart His call to prayer; yield to Him today by presenting more requests to Him, for more of the saints.

Day Fourteen

ELEMENTS OF SPIRITUAL PRAYER

In *Keep in Step with the Spirit*, J. I. Packer lists four elements of spiritual prayer:

> First it is a matter of seeking, claiming, and making use of access to God through Christ (Ephesians 2:18).
>
> Then the Christian adores and thanks God for his acceptance through Christ and for the knowledge that through Christ his prayers are heard.
>
> Third, he asks for the Spirit's help to see and do what brings glory to Christ, knowing that both the Spirit and Christ himself intercede for him…(Romans 8:26–27, 34).
>
> Finally, the Spirit leads the believer to concentrate on God and his glory in Christ with a sustained, single-minded simplicity of attention and intensity of desire…supernaturally wrought.

May each of these bring you new spiritual intensity.

P . R . A . Y . FOR TODAY

Praise God for accepting you through Christ;
repent of any failure to use your access to God through
Christ; ask for His Spirit's power in living this day in
integrity; yield to Him by doing what is right wherever
you've been tempted to do otherwise.

RISING UPWARD IN PRAYER

In his *Institutes of the Christian Religion,* John Calvin taught believers that those who pray should "rise to a purity worthy of God" and should be "so impressed with the majesty of God that they engage in it free from all earthly cares and affections":

> The ceremony of lifting up our hands in prayer is designed to remind us that we are far removed from God, unless our thoughts rise upward; as it is said in the psalm, "Unto thee, O LORD, do I lift up my soul" (Psalm 25:1). And Scripture repeatedly uses the expression to *raise our prayers,* meaning that those who would be heard by God must not grovel in the mire.

It's our privilege to not only raise our hands in worship but also to combine the visible with the invisible in a rising stream of praise and adoration sent directly to our Father.

P.R.A.Y. for Today

Praise God for His splendor and purity;
repent of any failure to be reverent in prayer and behavior;
ask for the Holy Spirit's help in rising above earthly
concerns; yield to Him by lifting up your hands as a
sign of lifting up your soul.

SINCERITY AND THE SPIRIT

John Bunyan, author of *The Pilgrim's Progress,* calls our attention to sincere prayer:

> What is prayer? A sincere, sensible, affectionate pouring out of the soul to God through Christ, in the strength and assistance of the Spirit, for such thing as God hath promised....
>
> While men are praying, God is searching the heart to see what is the meaning of the Spirit, or whether there be the Spirit and his meaning in all that the mouth hath uttered, either by words, signs, or groans, because it is by him and through his help only that any make prayers according to the will of God (Romans 8:26–27).

Praying effectively requires the intervention of God's Holy Spirit. Through the intentions of our hearts and the engagement of the Spirit, we discover the will of God.

P.R.A.Y. for Today

*Praise God for understanding your prayers even
when you're unable to express them in words;
repent of disregarding the Holy Spirit's part,
and for speaking mindlessly or insincerely;
ask Him to teach you how to pray more surely;
yield by remaining quiet before Him, listening, in prayer.*

A TIMELESS PERSPECTIVE

As the first world war raged in Europe, P. T. Forsyth noted in *The Soul of Prayer* how people had developed deeper interest in prayer. But in a chapter called "The Timeliness of Prayer," Forsyth addressed a larger frame of reference:

> The real power of prayer in history...is the corporate action of a Saviour-Intercessor and His community, a volume and energy of prayer organized in a Holy Spirit and in the Church the Spirit creates.... True prayer...is in the most organic and vital context of affairs, private and public, if all things work together, deeply and afar, for the deep and final kingdom of God.

In times of conflict we naturally pray for peace on earth. Yet in God's righteous and final judgment, the problems of this life will quickly fall away. Our only concern then will be for our citizenship in His eternal kingdom in heaven.

P. R. A. Y. FOR TODAY

Praise God for His sovereignty over our world,
and for His assured victory over evil;
repent of any fear of evil that you've had or any failure to
trust Him; ask for His peace; yield to Him by offering
encouragement to others who seem fearful or insecure.

BATTLE-MINDED PRAYER

In *The Pleasures of God,* after John Piper points to our need to be faithful to our Christ-given mission on the battlefield of world evangelism, he writes:

> The crying need of the hour—every hour—is to put the churches on a wartime footing.... How will the church ever come to think this way? How will millions of lukewarm church-goers be brought to wartime readiness and put on military alert?...
>
> I believe the answer, beneath and behind the renewed empowering of the Word of God, is a movement of persevering, believing, expectant prayer.... And only when the people of God "cry to him day and night" will God come forth with power and vindicate his cause in the world.

As we join together in prayer, we draw on God's enabling might in a way that multiplies our own efforts many times over. We *will* succeed in bringing God's Word to the world when we pray together in His holy name!

P.R.A.Y. for Today

Praise God for victory in the world; repent of any failure by your church to be battle-minded; ask for His particular battle strategies for you and your church at this time; yield to Him in willingness to be His soldier.

THE DEVIL'S TACTICS

In C. S. Lewis's *The Screwtape Letters,* Screwtape counsels Wormwood on ways to keep Christians from praying to God:

> The simplest is to turn their gaze away from Him towards themselves. Keep them watching their own minds and trying to produce *feelings* there by the action of their own wills. When they meant to ask Him for charity, let them, instead, start trying to manufacture charitable feelings for themselves and not notice that this is what they are doing. When they meant to pray for courage, let them really be trying to feel brave. When they say they are praying for forgiveness, let them be trying to feel forgiven. Teach them to estimate the value of each prayer by their success in producing the desired feeling.

Mind, will, and emotion all belong to the soul. All the more reason to pray entirely "in the Spirit."

P.R.A.Y. FOR TODAY

Praise God for His power; repent of any ways you've tried to manufacture feelings; ask God for true love, true courage, true forgiveness; yield to Him by putting no stock in your negative feelings.

Day Twenty

WARFARE PRAYING

Pastor and author Tony Evans, in *The Battle Is the Lord's,* summarizes a biblical outline "for the kind of spiritual warfare praying that brings down satanic strongholds":

> There must be agreement and unity, we must come together in Jesus' name, and we need to focus on Him, bringing Him into the midst of our prayer circle.
>
> When we do that, and then act in light of God's comprehensive revealed Word, including the application of the revelatory aspects of the Old Testament law, we'll see prayers answered. We'll have power to affect the community that we never thought possible. When Jesus is in our midst, He brings His limitless power along as well. But…Jesus must be in the middle, all eyes and hearts focused on Him.

Pray in Christ's name, for Satan has no power against it.

P.R.A.Y. for Today

Praise God for His promised victory in our spiritual warfare; repent of any failure by your church to make Jesus its focus; ask Him to shake your community, your nation, and the world; yield to Him by praying for this in unity with other believers.

PRAYING FOR HOLINESS

In *The Pursuit of Holiness,* Jerry Bridges teaches that we should express our dependence on the Holy Spirit by praying for holiness:

> The Apostle Paul prayed continually for the working of God's Spirit in the lives of those to whom he was writing. He told the Ephesians that he prayed God would "strengthen you with power through His Spirit in your inner being" (Ephesians 3:16). He prayed that God would fill the Colossians "with the knowledge of His will through all spiritual wisdom and understanding" so that they might "live a life worthy of the Lord and may please Him in every way" (Colossians 1:9–10).

Holiness should be a constant goal for all of us. That we might never achieve it in our natural lifetime is not the point. Christ prepares us for the perfection of heaven by lessening the imperfections of earth.

P.R.A.Y. FOR TODAY

Praise God for His holiness, His transcendent majesty;
repent of any impurity in your actions, thoughts,
and words; ask for His Spirit's help in making progress
in holiness today; yield to Him by obeying in the specific
areas He brings to mind.

Day Twenty-two

FAITH IN GOD

When Jesus cursed a fig tree and it withered, He used the occasion to teach His disciples first about faith, and then about prayer.

> "Have faith in God," Jesus answered. "I tell you the truth, if anyone says to this mountain, 'Go, throw yourself into the sea,' and does not doubt in his heart but believes that what he says will happen, it will be done for him. Therefore I tell you, whatever you ask for in prayer, believe that you have received it, and it will be yours." (Mark 11:22–24)

As Andrew Murray notes in *With Christ in the School of Prayer,* "The power to believe *a promise* depends entirely, but only, on faith in *the promiser.* Trust in the person begets trust in his word."

Just as our faith strengthens our prayer life, so do our prayers deepen our faith. Let us pray often, starting today, for a deeper, more powerful faith.

P.R.A.Y. for Today

Praise God for His ability to move mountains;
repent of any mountain of sin or distrust in your life;
ask God to remove that mountain;
yield to Him by doing your part to remove it.

OPENING HIS BOOK

In his *Confessions*, Augustine addressed the entire text to God—making it, in essence, a book-length prayer. Here, Augustine prays for his partaking of God's Word:

> Yours is the day, yours the night. No moment of time passes except by your will. Grant me some part of it for my meditations on the secrets of your law. Do not close your door to those who knock: do not close the book of your law to me…. O Lord, perfect your work in me. Open to me the pages of your book…. Let me acknowledge as yours whatever I find in your books. Let me listen to the sound of your praises. Let me drink you in and contemplate the wonders of your law.

> May each of us pray the same prayer, that God by His own grace would open each of our hearts, in a personal way, to the wonders of Himself.

P.R.A.Y. FOR TODAY
*Praise God for His wonderful Word;
repent of any failure to listen to Him in His Word;
ask for Him to open up His Word to your heart;
yield to Him by spending concentrated time
in His Word today.*

PRAYER AND GODLINESS

In *The Practice of Godliness,* Jerry Bridges defines godliness as both "God-centeredness, or devotion to God; and Godlikeness, or Christian character." Both aspects will flourish through our prayers.

> As we concentrate on growing in our reverence and awe for God and in our understanding of His love for us, we will find that our desire for Him will grow. As we gaze upon His beauty we will desire to seek Him even more. And as we become progressively more aware of His redeeming love, we will want to know Him in a progressively deeper way. But we can also pray that God will deepen our desire for Him.

> God lovingly provides the means for us to continually expand our reverence for Him. The secret to tapping into that source, as always, is prayer.

P.R.A.Y. for Today

*Praise God for being infinitely glorious,
and for implanting within you a deep desire to know Him;
repent of the times when your desire to know Him has
seemed weak; ask Him to strengthen your desire to know
Him; yield to Him by reading in His Word and waiting
quietly for His presence to be made known to you.*

PRAYING FOR OUR ENEMIES

Hear the words of Jesus to all who would follow Him: "I tell you: Love your enemies and pray for those who persecute you" (Matthew 5:44).

For the German pastor and theologian Dietrich Bonhoeffer, the enemy was obvious—he was imprisoned and finally murdered by the Nazis. Facing this persecution, he had these comments on Christ's directive to love our enemies:

> This is the supreme demand. Through the medium of prayer we go to our enemy, stand by his side, and plead for him to God. Jesus does not promise that when we bless our enemies and do good to them they will not despitefully use and persecute us. They certainly will. But not even that can hurt or overcome us, so long as we pray for them.

God does amazing works through prayers that seek to extend His grace to others. Truly, God's grace knows no bounds!

P.R.A.Y. for Today

Praise God for loving us even when we were His enemies;
repent of any bitterness you've held toward others;
ask for God's blessings on your enemies;
yield to Him by seeking to do good to these people.

CONQUERED BY GOD

In *The Divine Conquest: God's Pursuit of Man*, A. W. Tozer writes:

> We might well pray for God to invade and conquer us, for until He does, we remain in peril from a thousand foes…. The strength of our flesh is an ever present danger to our souls. Deliverance can come to us only by the defeat of our old life. Safety and peace come only after we have been forced to our knees. God rescues us by breaking us, by shattering our strength and wiping out our resistance. Then He invades our natures with that ancient and eternal life which is from the beginning. So He conquers us and by that benign conquest saves us for Himself.

God conquers only what we yield to Him—yet when He does, and when our surrender is complete, He fills us with a new strength that we could never have known by ourselves. His conquest is our victory!

P.R.A.Y. FOR TODAY
*Praise God for conquering your soul;
repent of any reliance on the strength of your flesh;
ask Him to shatter your self-reliance;
yield to Him by casting it off.*

EMPTY OF SELF, FULL OF GOD

In John 15:5, Jesus said, "Apart from me you can do nothing."

When he was a young man, John Wesley wrote to his mother:

> My desire is to know and feel that I am nothing, that I have nothing, and that I can do nothing. For whenever I am empty of myself, then know I of a surety that neither friends nor foes, nor any creature, can hinder me from being "filled with all the fullness of God."

The nothingness Wesley talks about may be the most elusive of all attributes. It defies the very "essence of self" on which so many of us base our identities. Yet when we give ourselves wholly to God, He takes from our meager reserves and gives back from infinity. What a marvelous exchange!

P.R.A.Y. FOR TODAY
Praise God for His fullness;
repent of your own fullness of self;
ask Him to fill you with His fullness;
yield to Him by emptying your mind
and spirit of every aspect of self.

ANSWERED PRAYER AND DELIBERATE SIN

Does God answer the prayers of a Christian who deliberately sins? When asked that question, theologian R. C. Sproul responded this way:

> When we refer to Christians who deliberately sin, we're talking about every Christian who ever lived, and we're talking about something that Christians do every day of their lives. We can talk about sins that are committed in ignorance and so on, but I hope we recognize that the vast majority of the sins we commit are done deliberately. We sin because we want to, because we choose to.
>
> If God refused to hear the prayers of Christians who deliberately sinned against him and then repented, God would not be listening to very many prayers. But we have the promise of God: *If we truly repent,* He will forgive us.

P.R.A.Y. for Today

*Praise God for knowing everything about you;
repent by acknowledging how often you want to
sin and choose to sin; ask Him to help you better
understand the ways you deceive yourself about your sin;
yield to Him by claiming and enjoying His forgiveness.*

IN THE DEPTHS OF THE VALLEY

Read this Puritan model of repentant, yielding prayer:

> Lord, high and holy, meek and lowly,
>   Thou hast brought me to the valley of vision,
> where I live in the depths but see thee in the heights;
>   hemmed in by mountains of sin I
>   behold thy glory.
> Let me learn by paradox
>   that the way down is the way up,
> that to be low is to be high,
>   that the broken heart is the healed heart,
> that the contrite spirit is the rejoicing spirit,
>   that the repenting soul is the victorious soul,
> that to have nothing is to possess all,
>   that to bear the cross is to wear the crown,
> that to give is to receive,
>   that the valley is the place of vision.

These simple truths form the heart of godly wisdom. Pray that they will take root in your heart today.

P.R.A.Y. FOR TODAY

Praise God for being "high and holy, meek and lowly";
repent of any sins of discouragement or despair;
ask for the riches of His joy; yield to Him by throwing
off gloom and taking on a rejoicing spirit.

PRAYER FOR SOMETHING NEW

On October 27, 1949, a Wheaton College student named Jim Elliot wrote in his journal:

> I have just now prayed for God's New Revelation—this generation's *real* laying hold of the Old Revelation. The old is become so undefined, so "accepted," so followed in blindness, that when the truth of it is brought to light, it shall be as a *new* revelation. I have prayed for new men, fiery, reckless men, possessed of uncontrollably youthful passion—these lit by the Spirit of God. I have prayed for new words, explosive, direct, simple words. I have prayed for *new miracles*.

On the next day he added a sentence that would become famous after his martyrdom in Ecuador in 1956: "He is no fool who gives what he cannot keep to gain that which he cannot lose."

May the inspired, eternal truth of that statement resonate within your heart.

P.R.A.Y. FOR TODAY

Praise God for His compassionate mercies; repent of any ways in which you've been stuck in old ruts; ask for new miracles from God; to gain what you cannot lose, yield to Him by giving up something you can't keep anyway.

GLORIFYING THE LORD

Jesus said, "I will do whatever you ask in my name, so that the Son may bring glory to the Father" (John 14:13). How should those words affect our prayer? Tony Marshall Anderson addressed that question in *Prayer Availeth Much:*

> Jesus revealed His purpose in answering prayer when He said, "…that the Father may be glorified in the Son." In order to achieve His exalted purpose to glorify the Father, the Son has bestowed on His redeemed people the inalienable right to ask anything in His Name. In the clear light of this remarkable truth…the possibilities in prayer are as great as the purpose of the Son of God.

> Pray daily that the Father might be further glorified in the Son through *your* life, too.

P.R.A.Y. FOR TODAY

Praise and thank God for allowing you to be His partner in ministry in this world; repent of any failure to step out boldly in ministry, empowered by Him; ask that the Father may be glorified in the Son through your ministry; yield to Him by expanding your outreach at this time, in dependence upon Him.

Endnotes

CHAPTER 1

Panic attack statistic from Martin Anthony, "Understanding Anxiety: Effects on Mental and Physical Health," symposium at Oregon Convention Center, 24 May 2001, Portland, Oregon.

Anxiety disorder statistic from the National Institute of Mental Health, "Facts about Anxiety Disorders," January 1999. http://www.nimh.nih.gov/anxiety/adfacts.cfm (accessed 17 December 2001).

Medical office visit statistic from Anne G. Perkins, "Medical Costs," *Harvard Business Review* 72, no. 6 (November/December 1994): 12.

Children's environment statistic from UNICEF, "The State of the World's Children 2000," 2000. http://www.childrenshour.org/how_ymh/statistics.html (accessed 17 December 2001).

CHAPTER 2

"I find that my worship is richer" from Ruth Myers with Warren Myers, *31 Days of Praise* (Sisters, Ore.: Multnomah Publishers, 1994), 25.

CHAPTER 3

"Sometimes it happens" from Elisabeth Elliot, *On Asking God Why* (Old Tappan, N.J.: Fleming H. Revell, 1989), 130.

CHAPTER 5

"The choice for me" from Lisa Beamer, remarks at Women of Faith conference, 9 November 2001, Philadelphia, Pennsylvania.

"Lay aside this ardor of mind" from Francois Fenelon, *Selections from the Writings of Francois Fenelon,* arranged and edited by Thomas S. Kepler (Nashville, Tenn.: Upper Room, 1962), 18–9.

31 DAYS TO P.R.A.Y.

Day 2, Robert L. Thomas, *1 Thessalonians,* in volume 11 of *The Expositor's Bible Commentary* (Grand Rapids, Mich.: Zondervan, 1978), 291.

Day 3, Robert E. Coleman, *The Master Plan of Evangelism* (Old Tappan, N.J.: Fleming H. Revell, 1963), 73.

Day 4, John G. Mitchell, *Fellowship: A Devotional Study of the Epistles of John* (Portland, Ore.: Multnomah Press, 1974), 14.

Day 5, Jim Cymbala with Dean Merrill, *Fresh Wind, Fresh Fire* (Grand Rapids, Mich.: Zondervan, 1997), 25, 50.

Day 6, Henry T. Blackaby and Claude V. King, *Experiencing God* (Nashville, Tenn.: Broadman & Holman, 1994), 174.

Day 7, Martin Luther, *Table Talk,* from the nineteenth-century translation by William Hazlitt (Philadelphia: Lutheran Publication Society), selection 329.

Day 8, William Law, *A Serious Call to a Devout and Holy Life* (1729), from chapter 14.

Day 9, E. M. Bounds (1835–1913), *Power through Prayer,* from chapter 19, "Deliberation Necessary to Largest Results from Prayer."

Day 10, Charles Haddon Spurgeon, *Morning and Evening: Daily Readings,* from the evening reading for October 8.

Day 11, Oswald Chambers, *If You Will Ask* (Grand Rapids, Mich.: Discovery House Publishers, 1985; copyright © 1958 by Oswald Chambers Publications Association Limited; U.S. copyright © 1985 by Chosen Books), 53–4.

Day 12, John Calvin, *Commentaries,* translated and edited by Joseph Haroutunian in collaboration with Louise Pettibone Smith (Philadelphia, Penn.: Westminster, 1958), commentary on John 7:38.

Day 13, R. A. Torrey, *How to Pray* (1900), from chapter 1, "The Importance of Prayer."

Day 14, J. I. Packer, *Keep in Step with the Spirit* (Old Tappan, N.J.: Fleming H. Revell), 79.

Day 15, John Calvin, *Institutes of the Christian Religion* (1845 edition translated by Henry Beveridge), book 3, chapter 20, sections 4–5.

Day 16, John Bunyan, from "Preparation for Prayer" in *Selections from the Writings of John Bunyan,* arranged and edited by Thomas S. Kepler (Nashville, Tenn.: Upper Room, 1951), 14–5.

Day 17, P. T. Forsyth, *The Soul of Prayer* (Grand Rapids, Mich.: Eerdmans, 1916), from chapter 4, "The Timeliness of Prayer."

Day 18, John Piper, *The Pleasures of God* (Portland, Ore.: Multnomah Press, 1991), 233, 235–6.

Day 19, C. S. Lewis, *The Screwtape Letters* (New York: Macmillan, 1945), 25–6.

Day 20, Tony Evans, *The Battle Is the Lord's* (Chicago: Moody Press, 1998), 403.

Day 21, Jerry Bridges, *The Pursuit of Holiness* (Colorado Springs, Colo.: NavPress, 1978), 79.

Day 22, Andrew Murray, *With Christ in the School of Prayer* in *The Deeper Christian Life and Other Writings,* Nelson's Royal Classics edition (Nashville, Tenn.: Thomas Nelson Publishers, 2000), 123.

Day 23, Augustine, *Confessions,* translated by R. S. Pine-Coffin (New York: Penguin Classics, 1961), 113.

Day 24, Jerry Bridges, *The Practice of Godliness* (Colorado Springs, Colo.: NavPress, 1983, revised 1996), 53.

Day 25, Dietrich Bonhoeffer, *The Cost of Discipleship* (New York: Macmillan, 1963; translated from the German *Nachfolge,* first published 1937; first English edition published 1949; second edition © SCM Press Ltd. 1959), 166.

Day 26, A. W. Tozer, *The Divine Conquest: God's Pursuit of Man* (Camp Hill, Penn.: Christian Publications, 1950), 57.

Day 27, John Wesley, letter to his mother, August 17, 1733, as quoted in *Selections from the Letters of John Wesley,* arranged and edited by J. Manning Potts (Nashville, Tenn.: Upper Room, 1952), 12–3.

Day 28, R. C. Sproul, *Now That's a Good Question!* (Wheaton, Ill.: Tyndale, 1996), 213.

Day 29, "Valley of Vision" in *The Valley of Vision: A Collection of Puritan Prayers & Devotions,* edited by Arthur Bennett (Edinburgh: Banner of Truth Trust, 1975), xv.

Day 30, Jim Elliot, *The Journals of Jim Elliot,* edited by Elisabeth Elliot (Old Tappan, N.J.: Fleming H. Revell, 1978), 173–4.

Day 31, Tony Marshall Anderson, *Prayer Availeth Much* (Circleville, Ohio: Advocate Publishing House, n.d.), from chapter 4, "The Praying that Glorifies God."

TIMELESS TRUTH
IN TEN MINUTES OR LESS

978-1-4143-1749-6

This award-winning daily devotional for couples from Dr. James and Shirley Dobson brings you personal, practical, and biblical insights that will renew your marriage—tonight and every night.

978-1-4143-1751-9

The Dobsons follow up their original best seller with another classic devotional. Discover a daily dose of emotional and spiritual insights for parenting children of all ages.

NATIONAL DAY OF PRAYER

The National Day of Prayer is a vital part of our heritage and provides an incredible opportunity for influence in the twenty-first century. By uniting with the body of Christ and participating in this annual event on the first Thursday of May, we become **"a city on a hill [that] cannot be hidden"** (Matthew 5:14).

Will you stand with us in lifting America and its leaders before God's throne?

Would you like to participate in a National Day of Prayer event in your community?

Sign up at our Web site: www.nationaldayofprayer.org.

For more information about the National Day of Prayer, call toll-free at 1-800-444-8828 or visit our Web site:

www.nationaldayofprayer.org.

CP0242